Moving Van Christmas

An original story about something that really happened on Christmas Day 2006

Mary "Corky" Treacy Thompson

For Cy and Bracken who were there,

and for Kaile, Tyler, Spencer,

Christian and Catherine

who weren't there,

but might enjoy this story anyway

Love and God bless,

Grandma

On Wednesday, it snowed.
It snowed and snowed and
snowed some more.
On Thursday, it was still
snowing.

The wind blew.
It blew some more.
The weather got
colder and colder.
The snow drifted and
drifted and drifted.

On Friday the airport in
Denver closed.
Planes couldn't fly.
Trains slowed and stopped.
The highways piled
high with snow.
People stayed at home.
They couldn't drive
anywhere.
The weatherman called
it a blizzard.

On a quiet street, a family was moving.
On Thursday, a big van
had come to help them.
Other people were getting
ready for Christmas, but this
family had packed
all their belongings.
They were waiting for the
moving man
to take their things.

But the snow
was everywhere.
The man couldn't carry the
boxes down the porch steps
and across the sidewalk
to the truck.
He had to lock his
truck and go to a
motel to sleep.

Then it stopped snowing.
By Saturday the snowplows
had cleared off most of the streets.
The moving man came back.
He carried all the boxes
down the steps
and into the truck.
It took all day and even
some of Sunday.
It was Christmas Eve.

Finally, the man loaded
the last box. He climbed into
his truck to drive all
the way to Florida.
The family got into their car
to drive to their new home.
Everyone else in
Denver was asleep.
The man started his truck.
He slowly crept down
the snowy street.

He turned the corner.

The truck crept some more.

The snow crunched.

The moving van stopped.

The man pressed
on the gas pedal.

The engine roared.

The truck rocked.

The truck didn't move.

It was stuck in the snow
on Christmas Eve!

On Christmas morning the sun came out. Children in Denver opened their presents. In one house the children looked out. They saw the great big moving truck stuck in the middle of the road—right in front of their house.

The driver looked sad.

He was all alone on Christmas Day.

The children's daddy
looked out, too.
He wondered where the
moving man had slept. He
thought he was probably
hungry, so he made him a
cup of coffee. He brought it
out to the man.
Then he invited him
in to share their
Christmas breakfast.

The man smiled when he
saw their Christmas tree
and the toys the
children had opened.
He smelled all the delicious
food and saw that they had
even set an extra place
for him at the table.
He missed his family,
but he didn't feel
so alone anymore.

The man told them all about his family and the farm where he lived. Then he called them on his phone, and they all cried a little because they were so far apart. They felt better when he told them that a nice family was sharing their breakfast with him.

Soon a tow truck
came to help.
It heaved and pulled.
The moving van heaved
and stuck. Then the tow
truck heaved one more time.
With a mighty clank, the van
slid out of its snow drift
and started down the street.
Everybody waved good-bye
and called,
"Merry Christmas!"

The family in Denver will
never forget that Christmas.
Everyone had made
a new friend.
They had given one of the
best gifts of all.
They had made a stranger
very, very happy,
and they felt very happy too.

36370888R00020

Made in the USA
Lexington, KY
16 October 2014